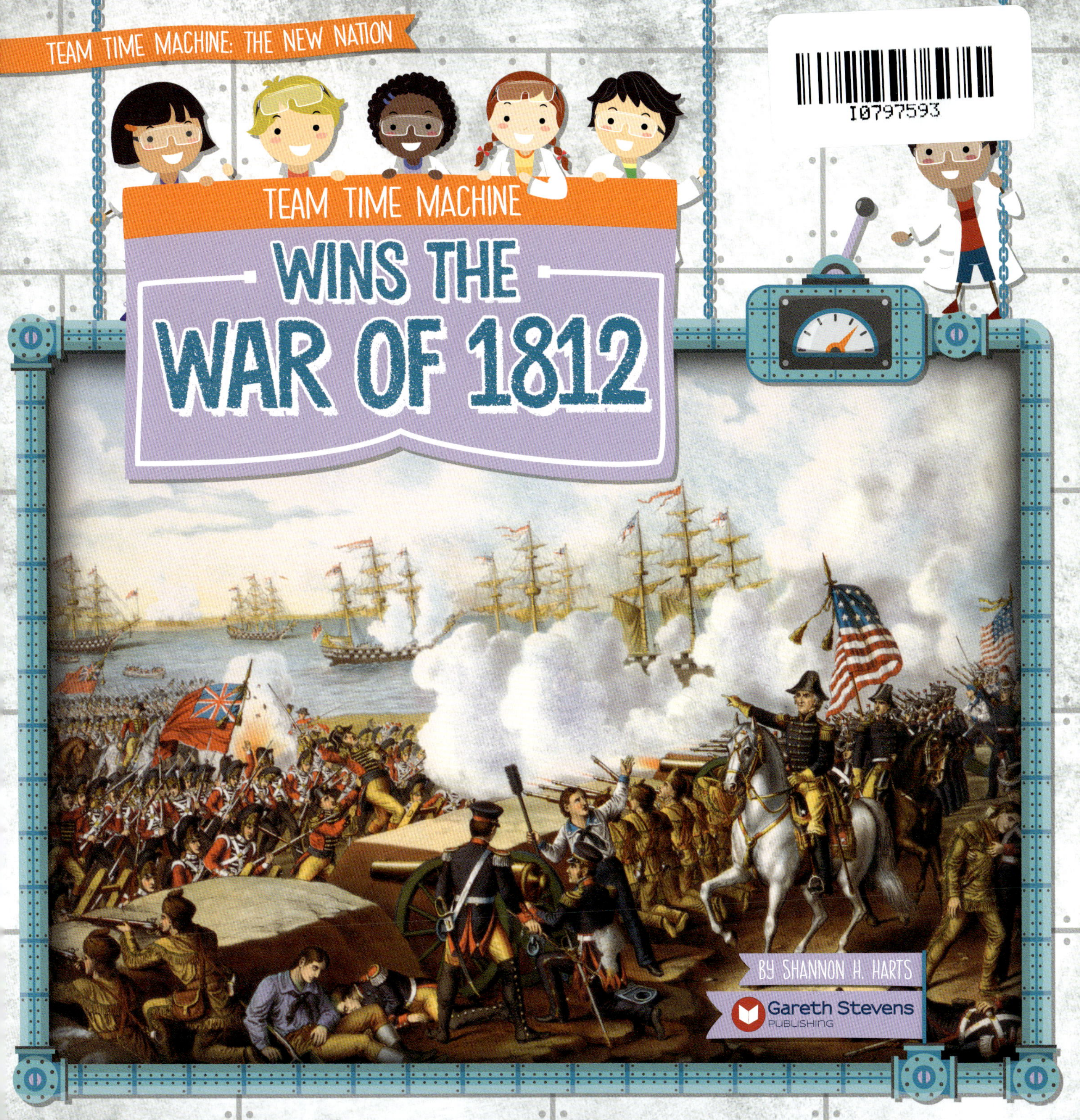
TEAM TIME MACHINE: THE NEW NATION
I0797593
TEAM TIME MACHINE
WINS THE
WAR OF 1812
BY SHANNON H. HARTS
Gareth Stevens
PUBLISHING

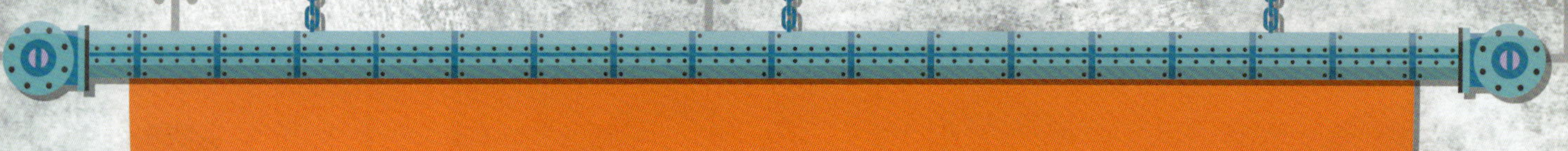

Please visit our website, www.garethstevens.com. For a free color catalog of all our high-quality books, call toll free 1-800-542-2595 or fax 1-877-542-2596.

Library of Congress Cataloging-in-Publication Data

Names: Harts, Shannon H., author.
Title: Team Time Machine Wins the War of 1812 / Shannon H. Harts.
Description: New York : Gareth Stevens Publishing, [2021] | Series: Team Time Machine: The New Nation | Includes index.
Identifiers: LCCN 2020003506 | ISBN 9781538257173 (library binding) | ISBN 9781538257159 (paperback) | ISBN 9781538257166 (6 Pack) | ISBN 9781538257180 (ebook)
Subjects: LCSH: United States--History--War of 1812--Juvenile literature.
Classification: LCC E354 .H373 2021 | DDC 973.5/2--dc23
LC record available at https://lccn.loc.gov/2020003506

First Edition

Published in 2021 by
Gareth Stevens Publishing
111 East 14th Street, Suite 349
New York, NY 10003

Designer: Katelyn E. Reynolds
Editor: Therese Shea

Photo credits: Cover, pp. 1, 17 (inset) Universal History Archive/Universal Images Group via Getty Images; cover, pp. 1–24 (series characters) Lorelyn Medina/Shutterstock.com; cover, pp. 1–24 (time machine elements) Agor2012/Shutterstock.com; cover, pp. 1–24 (background texture) somen/Shutterstock.com; p. 5 (main) Stephen Dunn/Getty Images; p. 5 (inset) Mormegil/Wikipedia.org; p. 7 The Print Collector/Print Collector/Getty Images; pp. 9, 25 Bettmann/Getty Images; pp. 11, 21 (main), 29 DeAgostini/Getty Images; p. 13 The Picture Art Collection / Alamy Stock Photo; p. 15 (main) Buyenlarge/Getty Images; p. 15 (inset) © Historical Picture Archive/CORBIS/Corbis via Getty Images; p. 17 (main) Charles Phelps Cushing/ClassicStock/Getty Images; p. 19 Fine Art Images/Heritage Images/Getty Images; p. 21 (map) Rainer Lesniewski/Shutterstock.com; p. 23 Cora Rosenhaft/ Moment Mobile/Getty Images; p. 27 History Archive/Universal Images Group via Getty Images.

Printed in the United States of America

CPSIA compliance information: Batch #CS20GS: For further information contact Gareth Stevens, New York, New York at 1-800-542-2595.

WORDS IN THE GLOSSARY APPEAR IN **BOLD** TYPE THE FIRST TIME THEY ARE USED IN THE TEXT.

CHAPTER 1: THE SEARCH FOR A SONG

"You've got this, Mia!" Sam shouted. Sam and Ben were in the stands at the ball field. They were about to watch their friend Mia play softball. A woman's voice sang "The Star-Spangled Banner" over a loudspeaker.

When she was done, Sam asked, "Was that song written during the **American Revolution**?"

Ben answered, "We learned in class that it was from the War of 1812."

"I have to do a project about it," Sam said. "Do you want to learn about the song in person?"

Ben grinned. "Let's head to the library!"

MEET TEAM TIME MACHINE

TEAM TIME MACHINE IS A GROUP OF FRIENDS WHO FOUND A TIME MACHINE ONE DAY IN A VERY ODD LIBRARY. THEY DISCOVERED THAT BOOKS FROM THE LIBRARY COULD POWER THE MACHINE AND TRANSPORT THEM TO DIFFERENT PLACES AND TIMES. IN THIS ADVENTURE, MIA, BEN, AND SAM TRAVEL BACK TO THE WAR OF 1812!

"THE STAR-SPANGLED BANNER" IS SUNG BEFORE MANY SPORTING EVENTS IN THE UNITED STATES. THE 1918 **WORLD SERIES** MAY HAVE BEEN THE FIRST TO FEATURE THE SONG.

After the game, Mia agreed to help Ben and Sam learn more about "The Star-Spangled Banner." Ben found a book about the War of 1812 at the Team Time Machine library.

"Let's find out about the war," he suggested. "Hopefully we'll learn about the song along the way."

"That's a good idea," Mia said. "I know the war was between the United States and Great Britain, but not much else."

Ben slipped the book into a slot in the time machine and pulled the handle.

"Here we go!" Sam said. "Hang on!"

THE WAR OF 1812 CAME AFTER THE AMERICAN REVOLUTION. IT TESTED THE YOUNG U.S. NAVY OF ABOUT 12 SHIPS AGAINST THE BRITISH ROYAL NAVY, WHICH HAD HUNDREDS OF SHIPS.

CHAPTER 2: ALL ABOARD

The library shook until a small screen said: "June 22, 1807." When the kids opened the door, they found themselves on a swaying ship. Mia went back into the library. (From the outside, it now looked like a ship's cabin!) She pulled the book from the machine and noticed a bookmark. She read the page and rejoined her friends.

"We're on USS *Chesapeake* off the coast of Norfolk, Virginia," she told them. Suddenly something slammed into the ship!

"That's a cannonball from HMS *Leopard*!" a nearby sailor yelled.

THE BRITISH SHIP HMS *LEOPARD* ATTACKED THE AMERICAN SHIP USS *CHESAPEAKE*. THE BRITISH SAID THEY WERE LOOKING FOR SAILORS WHO HAD **DESERTED** THE BRITISH NAVY.

THE BRITISH IMPRESSMENT OF SAILORS ON AMERICAN SHIPS WAS ONE CAUSE OF THE WAR OF 1812. IMPRESSMENT MEANS FORCING PEOPLE TO JOIN THE MILITARY.

"Let's get out of here!" Sam shouted. The friends ran into the library. Mia stuck the bookmark into a new spot and placed the book in the time machine.

After another bumpy ride, they came out of a tent—onto a battlefield! Not too far away, they could see soldiers wearing red running after soldiers in blue.

"We're in Detroit, August 1812," Mia said. "The British are chasing back American troops that had **invaded** Canada. Great Britain owned Canada then."

THE UNITED STATES HAD **DECLARED** WAR AGAINST GREAT BRITAIN IN JUNE 1812. IMPRESSMENT OF U.S. SAILORS WAS ONE REASON. ANOTHER WAS THE BRITISH STOPPING U.S. TRADE SHIPS FROM REACHING EUROPE. SOME THOUGHT THE BRITISH TOLD NATIVE AMERICANS TO ATTACK U.S. SETTLEMENTS TOO.

GENERAL WILLIAM HULL LED U.S. SOLDIERS INTO CANADA FROM DETROIT, MICHIGAN, TO CAPTURE BRITISH TERRITORY. HOWEVER, HIS TROOPS WERE CHASED BACK. HULL **SURRENDERED** DETROIT ON AUGUST 16, 1812.

CHAPTER 4: BLAZES AT THE BATTLE OF YORK

Mia flipped more pages in the book and placed the bookmark again. "Okay! I have our next stop—the Battle of York—April 27, 1813."

The friends rushed into the tent that held the library. Mia put the book in the time machine. When they stepped out again, they were in a colonial city—on fire! People were running away from the smoke and flames.

A settler ran by them shouting, "Leave York, children! The Americans have won, but they're lighting buildings on fire!"

YORK IS IN PRESENT-DAY TORONTO, CANADA. AT THE TIME, IT WAS THE CAPITAL OF AN AREA CALLED UPPER CANADA. THIS AMERICAN VICTORY WAS A STEP FORWARD IN THE PLAN TO CAPTURE CANADIAN TERRITORY.

BEFORE THE BRITISH LEFT YORK, THEY LIT THE REMAINING GUNPOWDER ON FIRE SO AMERICANS COULDN'T USE IT. THE BLAST KILLED MANY AMERICANS, INCLUDING GENERAL ZEBULON PIKE.

CHAPTER 5: VICTORY ON LAKE ERIE

The team stepped back into the library and away from the danger. After time-traveling again, they arrived on a U.S. Navy ship, one of nine. Six British ships were sailing away. All had been **damaged** in battle.

"What's going on?" Sam asked an American sailor.

"We've won control of Lake Erie!" he replied proudly. "Oliver Hazard Perry led us to victory. When his ship was damaged, he rowed to another. Then he sailed right at the British! We fired until they surrendered."

WE HAD ARRIVED AT THE END OF THE BATTLE OF LAKE ERIE ON SEPTEMBER 10, 1813. THE AMERICAN VICTORY STOPPED THE BRITISH FROM TAKING MORE LAND IN THE PART OF THE UNITED STATES CALLED THE NORTHWEST TERRITORY.

OLIVER HAZARD PERRY LED THE AMERICANS AT THE BATTLE OF LAKE ERIE. HE WAS A MASTER COMMANDANT IN THE U.S. NAVY AND BECAME A CAPTAIN AFTER THE BATTLE.

OLIVER HAZARD PERRY

CHAPTER 6: TAKING A THAMES WIN

After the battle, the American naval ships carried the forces of General William Henry Harrison—and Team Time Machine—to Detroit. Harrison's troops took back the city from the British. Then they chased the British east. The kids followed partway by ship. They caught up with the army near Moraviantown in Canada, near the Thames River. There, the Battle of the Thames took place on October 5, 1813.

The kids watched as the outnumbered British soldiers and their Native American **allies** lost to the Americans.

THE SHAWNEE LEADER TECUMSEH DIED AT THE BATTLE OF THE THAMES. THIS RESULTED IN NATIVE AMERICANS LOSING LAND IN THE OHIO AND INDIANA TERRITORIES.

MAJOR GENERAL WILLIAM HENRY HARRISON LED ABOUT 3,500 TROOPS AT THE BATTLE OF THE THAMES AGAINST ABOUT 900 BRITISH SOLDIERS AND 500 NATIVE AMERICAN WARRIORS. HARRISON LATER BECAME THE NINTH U.S. PRESIDENT.

CHAPTER 7: CRISIS AT THE CAPITAL

After the battle, the kids walked back to their library hidden aboard the navy ship. Sam asked Mia for the book. He said, "There's another event in this war we should see." He moved the bookmark and put the book in the time machine. They arrived in the U.S. capital, Washington, DC, in August 1814.

"Isn't that the White House?" Mia asked, pointing. "It looks like it was burned!"

"What happened?" Ben asked a woman nearby.

"Didn't you hear?" she replied. "The British took control and set government buildings on fire!"

MONTHS BEFORE WASHINGTON, DC, BURNED, BRITISH TROOPS HAD SET FIRE TO MOST OF BUFFALO, NEW YORK. THIS CAME AFTER AMERICANS BURNED DOWN THE BRITISH VILLAGE OF NEWARK, TODAY'S TOWN OF NIAGARA-ON-THE-LAKE.

THE CAPITOL IS THE BUILDING WHERE CONGRESS MEETS IN WASHINGTON, DC. THE BRITISH SET IT ON FIRE AS WELL AS THE WHITE HOUSE AND OTHER IMPORTANT BUILDINGS. A RAINSTORM KEPT THE CITY FROM COMPLETE RUIN.

CHAPTER 8: A POWERFUL WIN AT PLATTSBURGH

Next, the three friends traveled ahead to September 11, 1814. They were once again on a ship, surrounded by 13 more U.S. ships. A sailor told them they were on USS *Ticonderoga* on Lake Champlain. More than 10,000 British troops were trying to invade New York from Canada. They had reached the town of Plattsburgh, New York.

The *Ticonderoga* faced off with 12 British ships over three hours. Team Time Machine hid as cannons fired. The American ships outmatched the British ships, forcing the British to **retreat**.

THE BATTLE OF PLATTSBURGH IS SOMETIMES CALLED THE BATTLE OF LAKE CHAMPLAIN. IT STOPPED BRITISH FORCES FROM TAKING NEW YORK THROUGH THE HUDSON RIVER VALLEY.

THE BATTLE OF PLATTSBURGH INCLUDED AROUND 4,000 U.S. SOLDIERS ON LAND WORKING TO KEEP BACK THE BRITISH FORCES. WITHOUT NAVAL SUPPORT, THE BRITISH FORCES HAD TO RETREAT.
CANADA
PLATTSBURGH
LAKE CHAMPLAIN
NEW YORK

CHAPTER 9: THE BRITISH AT BALTIMORE

"What a win!" Sam said after the battle. "We've seen so much of this war, but there's no sign of 'The Star-Spangled Banner' yet."

"One more try," Mia said, putting the bookmark on a new page. The team traveled to two days later, September 13, 1814. This time when they opened the library door, they were on a British ship.

"Where are we?" Ben asked a British sailor.

"Baltimore, Maryland," he replied. "We're on the attack!"

The sailor's voice could hardly be heard over the loud *booms* of firing cannons.

WE ARRIVED AT THE BATTLE OF BALTIMORE. DURING THE BATTLE, BRITISH WARSHIPS FIRED ON THE CITY'S FORT MCHENRY FOR AROUND 25 HOURS STRAIGHT!

THE BATTLE OF BALTIMORE WAS AN IMPORTANT PART OF THE WAR OF 1812. EVENTS ARE STILL REENACTED, OR ACTED OUT, WITH SHIPS LIKE THE *PRIDE OF BALTIMORE II*.

CHAPTER 10: AN ANTHEM IS BORN

Team Time Machine stayed on the British ship and watched for signs of surrender from Fort McHenry throughout the night. When a hint of dawn's light could be seen, Ben saw a man on the deck who wasn't dressed like a sailor. The man watched the American flag waving over the fort. He wrote on a piece of paper.

Ben asked, "What are you writing, sir?"

"A poem," he said, "about that star-**spangled** banner that yet waves."

Ben turned to Mia and Sam. He said, "Those are words from the song! Mystery solved!"

THE MAN ON THE SHIP WAS FRANCIS SCOTT KEY, AN AMERICAN LAWYER AND POET. HE HAD BEEN TRYING TO GET BRITISH OFFICERS TO SET AN AMERICAN PRISONER FREE.

ON SEPTEMBER 14, FRANCIS SCOTT KEY WROTE A POEM CALLED "DEFENCE OF FORT M'HENRY." HE WAS PROUD THE FORT HADN'T SURRENDERED. THE POEM BECAME A SONG THAT WAS ADOPTED AS THE U.S. NATIONAL **ANTHEM** "THE STAR-SPANGLED BANNER" IN 1931.

CHAPTER 11: THE TREATY OF GHENT

Team Time Machine made one more trip. They wanted to see how the War of 1812 ended. They traveled to Ghent, Belgium, on Christmas Eve in 1814.

Dressed as servants, they heard American and British leaders talking about ways to end the war. The United States wanted to end impressment of sailors. The British wanted to keep lands they had captured. Great Britain also wanted to end the war because they were fighting another war with France in Europe. A treaty, or agreement, was reached called the Treaty of Ghent.

ONE OF THE AMERICAN LEADERS SENT BY PRESIDENT JAMES MADISON TO GHENT WAS JOHN QUINCY ADAMS. THE SON OF JOHN ADAMS, HE WOULD BECOME PRESIDENT IN 1825.

NEWS OF THE TREATY TRAVELED SLOWLY. THE BRITISH TRIED TO TAKE NEW ORLEANS, LOUISIANA, IN JANUARY 1815. MAJOR GENERAL ANDREW JACKSON LED AMERICAN FORCES TO VICTORY. HE WOULD BE ELECTED U.S. PRESIDENT IN 1829.

CHAPTER 12: A NATION PROVES ITS POWER

"So, did the United States win this war?" Ben whispered to Mia and Sam. They were watching the leaders take turns signing the Treaty of Ghent.

"I don't know. Things are just going back to how they were before the war," Mia said.

"But now Great Britain sees the United States as a real country with power," Ben said.

"I think we're the winners for solving the song mystery!" Sam said. "Now let's get back so I can finish my project!"

AMERICANS DIDN'T GET THE BRITISH TO AGREE TO END IMPRESSMENT, AND GREAT BRITAIN KEPT TERRITORY IN CANADA. HOWEVER, AMERICANS BEGAN SETTLING IN LANDS ALONG THE GREAT LAKES.

WAR OF 1812 TIMELINE

1807

JUNE: HMS *LEOPARD* FIRES ON USS *CHESAPEAKE*.

1812

JUNE: THE UNITED STATES DECLARES WAR ON GREAT BRITAIN.

AUGUST: DETROIT IS SURRENDERED AFTER A FAILED AMERICAN INVASION OF CANADA.

AUGUST: USS *CONSTITUTION* DEFEATS HMS *GUERRIERE*.

1813

APRIL: U.S. SOLDIERS TAKE YORK IN PRESENT-DAY TORONTO.

SEPTEMBER: OLIVER HAZARD PERRY LEADS U.S. SHIPS TO VICTORY ON LAKE ERIE.

OCTOBER: TECUMSEH IS KILLED AT THE BATTLE OF THE THAMES.

DECEMBER: BRITISH FORCES TAKE FORT NIAGARA.

1814

JULY: A VICTORY AT THE BATTLE OF CHIPPEWA BOOSTS AMERICAN SPIRITS.

AUGUST: THE BRITISH BURN WASHINGTON, DC.

SEPTEMBER: THE BATTLE OF PLATTSBURGH STOPS AN INVASION OF NEW YORK.

SEPTEMBER: THE BRITISH ATTACK FORT MCHENRY. FRANCIS SCOTT KEY BEGINS THE POEM THAT BECOMES "THE STAR-SPANGLED BANNER."

DECEMBER: U.S. AND BRITISH LEADERS SIGN THE TREATY OF GHENT.

1815

JANUARY: ANDREW JACKSON LEADS A U.S. VICTORY AT THE BATTLE OF NEW ORLEANS.

FEBRUARY: THE SENATE AGREES TO THE TREATY OF GHENT, ENDING THE WAR.

SAM MADE THIS TIMELINE FOR HIS HISTORY PROJECT.

GLOSSARY

ally: one of two or more people or groups who work together

American Revolution: the war in which the colonies won their freedom from England

anthem: a song declaring loyalty to a group, cause, or country

damage: harm. Also, to cause harm

declare: to formally announce

desert: to leave military service without permission

invade: to enter a place to take it over

retreat: to move back or away from an attack or danger

spangled: sprinkled or decorated with

surrender: to give up

victory: a win over an opponent

World Series: the annual championship competition of Major League Baseball

FOR MORE INFORMATION

BOOKS

Alvarez, Pilar F. *The War of 1812: New Challenges for a New Nation.* New York, NY: PowerKids Press, 2017.

Hinman, Bonnie. *The War of 1812: 12 Things to Know.* Mankato, MN: 12-Story Library, 2016.

Orr, Tamra. *The Star-Spangled Banner: Introducing Primary Sources.* North Mankato, MN: Capstone Press, 2016.

WEBSITES

Oh Say Did You Know These 7 Facts About The Star-Spangled Banner?
www.pbs.org/newshour/arts/seven-facts-star-spangled-banner
Check out fun facts to share about "The Star-Spangled Banner."

US History: War of 1812
www.ducksters.com/history/us_1800s/war_of_1812.php
Find facts about causes, battles, and leaders of the War of 1812.

What Was the War of 1812?
www.wonderopolis.org/wonder/what-was-the-war-of-1812
Learn more about why this war is important to U.S. history.

INDEX